Beer for
Beginners

The Foremost Home Winemaking Series

General Editor: **B. C. A. Turner**

Kenneth Hill

Beer for Beginners

Mills & Boon LIMITED, LONDON

First published in Great Britain 1971 by
Mills and Boon Limited, 17–19 Foley Street, London
W1A 1DR

ISBN 0 263 51604 0

Made and printed in Great Britain by
C. Nicholls & Company Ltd
The Philips Park Press, Manchester. M11 4AU.

Contents

Preface

Why bother making beer at home? It is so easy to call at the supermarket down the road and these days there seems to be one in every road. There you can always pick up a container pack of six 8 oz bottles or cans of beer. We are living in an age of mass production in which the results are sold to us in such beautifully presented packages we become dazzled with their splendour and forget to examine the product inside. The liquid called beer is crystal-clear and almost flavourless. The present-day beers are being sold on eye appeal rather than on taste. Where are the full flavoured beers for which our country is famous? Lost or almost lost in the computerised continuous beer machines that are rapidly replacing the old-established breweries. Soon we will be left with only one beer throughout the country and that produced by a giant and soul-less corporation.

Fortunately you cannot fool all the people all the time. Like so many others, it suddenly dawned upon me that I was paying a fantastic price for a glass of semi-tasteless liquid. I was luckier than some. I appreciated these terrible facts a little quicker than most others and as result I started going around the few traditionally run breweries in the country. I studied their ways and methods. I read the many excellent books on traditional brewing that were produced by commercial brewers

over the years when quality was a motive
force. I coupled this with a natural love for
making something that could not be bought.
After many trials and errors I have reached the
point where I feel that I can in all honesty
produce a better flavoured pint of beer than
you can get in most pubs.

An additional side benefit is that my own beer
is so much cheaper. I can make a gallon for a
little over the cost of a pint of commercial
beer. All this despite the fact that quality
rather than cheapness has been my guiding
principle. Cheapness is brought about by bulk
buying of ingredients, but as far as quality
goes I always insist on the highest. Many home
brewers want only a cheap alcoholic drink
and, believe me, this is very easily obtained
with little or no effort in the field of home
brewing. But with a little extra effort so much
more can be achieved. By making your own
beer at home you can supply yourself with a
beer to suit your individual palate. In the same
way that a hand-made suit will fit you better,
so also will a well-made pint of home brew
refresh and stimulate you. Do not make it too
strong: remember the breath test, especially
when entertaining your friends. I hope that this
book helps you to return to the good old days
when home-made bread, farmhouse cheese
and a pint of home brew made life worth living.

1 History of Beer

To write the history of beer would take a book in itself. In this little book I can bring to your notice only some of the salient dates and records of events.

If ancient documents are to be believed, a type of grain drink was being made by the Egyptians some 3000 years B.C. It will no doubt bring joy to the hearts of the prohibitionists to know that among the ancient papers of Egyptian history there are complaints by the Egyptian officials against the growing number of ale shops on the grounds that there were already too many. Perish the thought!

In Great Britain grain drinks have been brewed since recorded history, the early drinks using honey as their source of sugar. The early drinks were always referred to as Ale. The word beer did not come into use until much later. The monasteries were at the forefront of the early breweries and as early as the year 1363 there are monastery records of a tax on the ale brewed. The records of the Priory of Worcester detail the making of ale in or about 1240. It is sad to relate that right from early times, the Government, whether national or local, appears to have taken great pains to extract as much money as it could from the brewers of ale. The only saving

grace from the consumer's point of view was
that the Government was just as interested in
the production of a brew of good quality.
Whether any present-day drinker tasting a
brew made similarly to that consumed in
olden days would find it to his liking is very
doubtful. Much of the early ale was from
malted wheat, oats and barley. Hops were not
in common use until introduced by Flemish
settlers around 1530. During the reign of
Richard III it was an offence to make ale in
which hops had been used and there are
records of persons being fined for brewing
ale with hops. Eventually hops became
universally accepted as a regular ingredient in
brewing.

The persons appointed by the Government to
check the quality of the ale were known as
Ale Conners. The post still exists today but is
purely titular. One of their early methods of
establishing the quality of the ale was to pour
a quantity onto a wooden bench outside the
premises and then to sit upon the ale in
leather breeches for about half an hour. If,
when the Ale Conner arose from the bench,
the breeches were stuck, the ale was
pronounced as being too full of sugar and
therefore of poor quality. Some authorities
have claimed that John Shakespeare, William's
father, was an Ale Conner.

Early recipes contained all sorts of weird and wonderful ingredients including such items as saltpetre, quassia chips and the roots of many vegetables. The main reason for these additions was that the ale had so many off-flavours that it required very strong added flavours to overcome them. Some ales were flavoured with heather, others with mountain ash berries, and even parsnips.

Nonetheless the drinking of ale seems to have been very popular, because in 1591 in Lancashire and Cheshire a complaint was made that during Church services the streets and ale shops were crowded and only the clergy were in the churches. Times do not seem to have changed much over the years. Recipes of the Middle Ages included elderberry ale, blackberry ale and cowslip ale. In these recipes the wort was a strong one (a hogshead of wort to a bushel of elderberries) and prior to fermenting the elderberries were boiled in it for half an hour. It was then strained and, when cool, yeast was added and it was fermented and casked. After a year in cask it was bottled. Blackberry ale was simpler. A strongly hopped ale wort was infused with the blackberries and fermented on the pulp. It was then strained and bottled and was supposed to be drinkable in three weeks. Cowslip ale was made similarly. I would not

personally recommend trying to emulate our
forebears unless you have a very strong
stomach and a liking for strong flavours.

Taken all round, the history of beer is a story
of continual restriction by Government, both
local and national, but despite this the trade
has survived. Right from the early days home
brewing was popular and I think that in the
next few years it is going to reach an all-time
peak.

2 Glossary of Terms

Alcohol
Obtained by the fermentation of sugar by the
apo-zymase complex of enzymes. The alcohol
so formed is 94% pure ethyl alcohol.

Acetic Acid
Colourless liquid contained in vinegar. It
develops as a result of the exposure to air of
the wort.

Attenuation
The lowering of the specific gravity of the
wort by fermentation.

Autolysis
The decomposition of dead yeast cells
releasing nitrogen for the use of living cells.
Causes off-flavours in the finished beer if not
removed by racking.

Calcium Sulphate
Found in Burton water and used in making
bitter beer. Adds tang. Useful additive to soft
water to make it harder.

Carageen Moss
An Irish seaweed added to boiling wort to
assist clarification of finished beer.

Caramel
Made by heating sugar until it darkens. Used
for colouring beers and stouts.

Condition
The amount of carbon dioxide gas in a
finished beer.

Dextrin
Unfermentable transparent gummy substance.
Has no taste or smell but gives body to a
finished beer.

Finings
Substance added to a finished beer to assist
clarification. Usually isinglass.

Flakes
Flaked maize or rice. Added to some grists
by commercial brewers, mainly for cheapness.
Flaked maize is said to give drier finish to
pale ale.

Glucose
Sugar formed by treating starch under slight
heat with weak solution of sulphuric acid.

Grist
Name to cover the different grains used in the
mashing of beer.

Head
The foam that forms on top of beer when
poured into a glass. The retention, which is so
much desired, can be improved by the dextrins
in the wort. Storage over 5 to 8 weeks also
improves head retention.

Hop Oil
The concentrate of oil in hops. Not recommended for home brewers. Commercial brewers use it at the rate of four drops to thirty-six gallons.

Isinglass
The bladder of sturgeons, when mixed with low acid solutions, forms a clearing solution.

Invert Sugar
Sugar that has been heated with a low acid solution. Ferments start the conversion to alcohol a little quicker than cane sugar.

Lactose
Milk sugar. Unfermentable by most yeasts. Added to brown beer or stouts to sweeten them.

Lees
Dead yeast and waste matter that collects on the bottom of a fermentation vessel during fermentation. Beer should be removed from lees by racking.

Liquor
Name given by commercial brewers to the water used in the making of beer.

Malt
Barley that has been heated in a moist atmosphere for approximately 14 days until

acrospire in barley grain develops. The barley
is then kiln-dried and the rootlets wither and
drop off. The starch in the barley has now
been converted to maltose which is readily
fermentable.

Malt Extract
Syrup obtained by evaporating extract of
mashed malted barley.

Mashing
The extraction of malt sugar from malted
barley by steeping it in water at between
145 and 152°F. For bitter beer 150°F (approx.).

Pitching
The addition of the yeast to wort.

Pitching Temperature
Temperature of wort at which yeast should be
pitched, 60°F.

Priming Sugar
The sugar added to a finished beer prior to
bottling to cause slight fermentation in beer.
Syrup made by dissolving one pound of sugar
in half a pint of water. Add one
teaspoonful per pint bottle.

Racking
Removal of beer from the lees by syphoning.

Rousing
The violent stirring of the beer to assist fermentation.

Sparging
The washing out of the mash grains by spraying liquor over the surface after having run off the original wort.

Striking Temperature
The temperature at which the mash grains (grist) are introduced into the liquor.

Tannic Acid
A constituent of hops, soluble in alcohol and water.

Wort
The crushed malted grains are mixed with liquor at a predetermined temperature until the starch in the grains is converted into fermentable sugar by the action of diastase. The resultant liquor is called the wort.

Bottom Yeast
Saccharomyces Carlsbergensis, used mainly on the Continent for attenuating the wort, the yeast remaining chiefly on the bottom of the vessel.

Top Yeast
Saccharomyces cerevisiae, used to attenuate the wort of British beers. The yeast rises to the top of the vessel.

3 Introduction to Home Brewing

Brewing beer at home has been in progress in Great Britain to a greater or lesser degree ever since the materials have been available. Just after the Second World War, when sugar could again be freely obtained, the hobby took on a new look. This was helped by Mr Reginald Maudling, the then Chancellor of the Exchequer, who in 1963 made it legal to brew as much beer as you wished in the home as long as you did not sell or barter the beer you made.

This allowed the home brewers to come out into the open and discuss their problems and improve their technique. Nowadays, in an age when all the big breweries are amalgamating and manufacturing a standardised product, there is even greater pleasure and benefit for the home brewer who can make beer to his or her individual taste. Brewing started off as a an art but has in the last century become a highly skilled science.

There are three ways of making beer at home and all have their adherents according to what you expect from your glass of beer. The more painstaking connoisseur whose aim is the best quality beer regardless of a little extra effort, and those who want to succeed in the big Regional or National beer competitions, make their beer in a method similar to the one used by the commercial brewer. This method is known as 'mashing' the malted barley. The second method, which will produce quite a drinkable beer and is one of the most popular, is making beer from malt extract. Lastly, there is a large following for making beer from 'beer packs'. These are ideal for people who do not wish to know anything about brewing. They can buy a composite pack with a few simple instructions and make quite a pleasant drink. The composition of these beer packs will obviously vary from supplier to supplier.

Whichever method you decide upon you can be safe in the knowledge that very little equipment will be necessary. Beer is a very personal drink. This is indicated by the number of breweries across the country, all producing beers of slightly different flavours and textures. I do not like to be dogmatic about which beer is best, precisely because it is so personal. I do feel, however, that it is unarguable that the home brew most universally accepted as the best, from the competition standpoint and from the opinion of commercial head brewers, is the one produced from mashing. This is not to say that makers of malt extract brews and beer pack brews will not defend their own products to the death, and to these people their own

beer IS best. If they like it best, then from
their standpoint it is the best. Home brew can
be placed in many categories but the main
ones are as follows.

Bitter Beer (Burton Type). This is a bitter
beer similar in style to those produced in
Burton-on-Trent and for which Burton is most
famous, e.g. Bass style or Double Diamond
style. In colour and taste these beers differ,
but from the point of alcoholic strength and
bitterness they are similar.

Light Ale. This is a bitter beer, lighter in
flavour, strength and bitterness than Burton
type. More like a dinner ale.

Mild Beer. This is brown, similar in style to
draught mild brown. It is lighter in flavour
than bottled brown beer.

Brown Beer. This is a bottled beer, but there
is no nationally known brown beer to compare
it with. The nearest description is similar to
Forest Brown. Usually fairly full-bodied,
slightly sweet and low-hopped.

Stout, Irish Style. This is obviously a bitter
stout similar in taste to GUINNESS.

Stout, Sweet. Stout similar to a milk stout

but not as bitter as Irish stout and with a sweet finish.

Oatmeal Stout. Not as bitter as Irish stout but not as sweet as sweet stout. A special flavour is imparted by the oatmeal.

Old Ale or Barley Wine. A high alcohol, dark brown beer, fairly sweet and with a higher hop rate than ordinary brown beer. Difficult to ferment out.

Lager. Continental style of bitter beer, clean on the palate, fairly low in hops. Ideally fermented out at very low temperature over several months. Use a bottom fermenting yeast. It is difficult to make the real lager but a reasonable substitute is feasible.

Many variations of the beer styles listed can be made, using any of the three methods, mashing, malt extract or beer packs. Before you make any beer by any method a sound knowledge of how beer is made and the various materials used must be acquired.

As home brewers we are very fortunate in that the commercial brewers have spent years researching into the best variety of barley to malt for beer making. For pale ale a malt that has a low nitrogen content is required, since this assists with the clarification of the beer.

As home brewers we have no choice in the
variety of malted barley that we purchase.
Nonetheless it is reassuring to know that
years of study have gone into producing the
ideal barley for malting. Moreover, the idea that
barley can be adequately crushed at home with
a rolling pin or a milk bottle must be rejected
from the outset. The brewer attaches great
importance to the degree to which the barley
is crushed. If crushed too finely it will congeal
like a dumpling when it comes in contact with
the liquor. If it is crushed too coarsely the
husks will not be sufficiently broken down for
the liquor to come in contact with the whole of
the interior of the barley kernel. From this it
will be appreciated that haphazard crushing
with a milk bottle will waste much time and in
the end between 25% and 30% only of the
grain will be crushed. In a commercial brewery
the grains are graded and run between rollers
of varying closeness, the larger grains being
directed between the rollers set at the greatest
distance apart. All the rollers are so set, that
the grain is crushed to break it down
sufficiently for the liquor to come into contact
with all the inside of the barley kernel,
without actually reducing it to flour.

I will describe the procedure at a commercial
brewery of the old school so that you can
follow the beer-making right through from

beginning to end. I have particularly chosen an older brewery as most modern breweries are so automated that the whole process is reduced to a man in charge of a large instrument panel. Clearly the romance is rapidly leaving modern breweries as the quest for greater profit increases.

Before describing the brewery, something must be said about malted barley, one of the most important factors in the making of good beer. The malted barley must not have a moisture content over 2%. This is more or less bone dry, so you must ensure that when you purchase your malt it is indeed perfectly dry and you must make every effort to keep it that way while you are storing it. If you fail the malt will become what is known as slack. This causes trouble in getting a good extract and you will encounter further difficulties in clearing the beer. For the regular beermaker I would suggest that you purchase your malt in bulk. I buy mine in 56 lb polythene bags. These are covered with a good quality sack and the whole is placed in a disused malt extract drum. Any other airtight container that is large enough will do. Make sure that you only open each sack long enough to take out the amount of malt that you intend to use. Then tie each bag tightly with string. Remember always to buy your malt already crushed.

Now to the brewery. The malt is collected on the top floor of the building in the malt store. The amount of grain to make up the grist for the forthcoming brew is crushed and mixed into a vessel below, called a malt hopper. Certain precautions are taken against any foreign bodies or metals getting into the grist, and against the danger of explosions from the dust and flour. On the lower floor is what is known as the grist case. This contains the crushed malted barley and any adjuncts that have gone into the mixture for the proposed brew. Immediately beneath the grist case is the mash tun. Into this mash tun is run the liquor which, you will remember, is the brewer's name for water. This water, as I have explained, used to conform to the style for a certain type of brew and came from wells. Nowadays, chemists are able to produce hard or soft water at will, by the use of chemical salts. Into the mash tun is injected either hard or soft water according to the type of beer to be brewed. This is heated to around 165°F (74°C), (known as the striking heat). The idea is that you want your mixture of malt and liquor to stabilise its temperature at a given point, e.g. for pale ales at between 150° and 152°F. So if you raise the temperature of the liquor above this, to, say, 165°F, then when the grain is mixed in it will bring the temperature down to the required 152°F.

The figure 152°F is known as the mashing temperature, and is a most significant figure as it is relevant to the making of all British pale ales. The effect of heated liquor on the crushed malt causes the saccharification of the starch in the malt grains and it is here that the temperature is so important. At 150°F and above the liquor extracts malt sugar known as maltose and, in addition, it extracts substances called dextrins. These are colourless, unsweetened, gummy substances which are tasteless. They give the beer body, and they are also believed to help with head retention. If you are making a high gravity beer then you must have the correct balance of dextrins.

The ratio of dextrins increases with the temperature from 150°F upwards. Lower down the scale if you mash at, say, 140°F, you would only extract maltose which is almost 100% fermentable. Consequently, if you are making pale ale similar to Bass or Double Diamond you should mash at approximately 152°F. The mixture in the mash tun is agitated internally for the first half hour and is then allowed to settle and remain undisturbed for an hour and a half. This is called 'standing on'. In the brewery the temperature is kept at 152°F for the whole of the two hours. The mash tun is fitted with a false bottom, so that after two

hours of standing on, the wort, as the liquor
is now called, is run off. At the same time
arms revolve inside the mash tun just above
the mash, through which more hot liquor
comes out in the form of a very fine spray. As
the sweet wort is run off through the spent
grains, which also act as a form of filter, the
sparge liquor, as it is called, is sprayed for
two more hours, washing through the grains
any sweetened wort still adhering to the
grains. The sparging liquor should be at
between 165° and 170°F so that the mash does
not fall below the mashing temperature of
152°F. The wort, still maintained at this
temperature, is collected in a vessel called an
underback.

The liquor is then pumped into the boiling
copper and invert sugar is added. The amount
of sugar used depends upon the style of beer
being brewed but is usually between 10% and
15% by weight of the total grist. Some of the
commercial sugars have caramel added,
according to the style of beer being brewed.
The hops are also added at this stage,
although some brewers add only about two
thirds of the quantity to be used at the
beginning of the boil, holding back the
remaining third to be added about fifteen
minutes before the end of the boil. In this way
they feel that they get a better extraction of

flavour from the hops. The boiling stage for the commercial brewer is of the greatest importance. Not only is he extracting all the essential oils and resins but he is also wanting to coagulate the protein matter in the wort. To achieve this the boil must be not only lengthy but also vigorous. A gentle simmer will be of no use whatsoever. The average length of a good vigorous boil is two hours. This sterilises the wort, extracts the resins and essential oils and coagulates the protein matter which assists in the later clarification of the brew.

Having completed the two-hour boil the wort is run off into the hop back. The hops sink to the bottom and form a filter bed. In the hop back the 'hop break' takes place. This is when the protein matter that has coagulated separates from the rest of the wort. The wort is now filtered through the hops and the bed is sparged with some boiling water to ensure that no wort is lost. The wort is pumped into the wort receiver and from there through a refrigeration plant such as a paraflow, i.e. thin pipes immersed In cold water. In the refrigeration plant the wort is cooled to 58°F and collected in the receiving vessels in the fermentation room.

The yeast is now pitched into the wort and

well mixed in so that after about 12 hours the
yeast bubbles start forming on the surface of
the wort. The early surface yeast contains
much waste matter such as small bits of hops
and other insolubles. It contains so much
impurity that it has to be skimmed off the
surface. The fermenting wort is roused from
time to time during the first three days of
fermentation. After the initial skimming of the
impure yeast the bubbles again collect on the
surface and form what is called a 'rocky head'.
The yeast bubbles rise up and form rock-like
shapes of froth and bubbles. As the
fermentation progresses the rocky head
settles down and is then skimmed off. A
further yeast head soon forms on the top of
the wort and acts as a protective screen to
the new beer beneath. By checking the fall in
gravity with a hydrometer the brewer can keep
a check on the rate of fermentation or, as
the brewers call it, the attenuation of the
brew.

One of the problems of the brewer during the
period of attenuation is to keep a close check
on the temperature of the wort. It will be
appreciated that if the air temperature is over
58°F then the wort in this atmosphere, plus the
heat generated by the activity of the yeast,
soon raises the temperature of the wort well
above the desired 58° to 60°F. This is overcome

by passing cold water through pipes in the fermentation vats to cool the wort. This is a point I feel is often overlooked by the home brewer who tends to attenuate at too high a temperature and may then complain that he sometimes gets a hard, acrid bitterness in his finished beer.

The system of attenuation I have just described varies throughout the country; different areas have their own special methods. Having attenuated out the alcohol required, the beer is now cleared. Bottle beers are often filtered through very efficient filters, while draught beer is run off into barrels and finings are added. The main aim is to remove the yeast deposits. There are still some commercial beers that are produced in the same way as the home brewed product. They are known as naturally fermented beers. This is how the bottled beer gets its carbon dioxide, not as the result of an injection of CO_2 gas, but from the gas released by natural fermentation in the bottle. The only pale ales on the market today that are made in this way are Red Triangle Bass and White Shield Worthington. They are not beloved of publicans because they need careful handling. Nonetheless they are still the best bottled beers available.

4 The Ingredients of Beer

1. Water

Beer is made from a mixture of grain, water, sugar and hops. From early times brewers discovered that water or, as it is known by the brewing industry, liquor, has an important part to play in beer making, particularly upon the style of beer. Why the brewers do not use the name water seems obscure; perhaps they refer to water as liquor because they do not like the popular idea that beer is watered. So from now on when I mention the word liquor I am, of course, meaning water. All the main breweries grew up around their water supplies. Thus London breweries, which centuries ago used Thames water, were famous for porter and other brown beers. Thames water in those days was clean and soft. In Burton-on-Trent the famous bitter beers were made. Their fame was due to the hard water of the Burton wells, which had a very high calcium sulphate content. Similarly, the Irish Liffey water, which was soft, proved to be ideal for stout making. Nowadays, of course, none of the water supplies from rivers would be fit to use. The facts remain the same. Hard water for bitter beer and soft water for browns and stouts. Home brewers can purchase salts to make water hard or soft according to their requirements, but to do the liquor preparation properly you should have the water that you normally use analysed. Having done this, a chemist could make up the salts to convert your local supply to the desired standard for hard or soft water.

Hard Burton-type liquor can have as much as 70 grains of calcium sulphate per gallon and 10 grains of magnesium sulphate. For stouts and brown beer approximately 10 grains of sodium chloride per gallon are necessary and no calcium sulphate. The style of liquor is more important to beer made from mashing the grain than to malt extract brews. There are many brewing today who feel that for the average home brewer with a water supply that is neither very hard nor very soft, their untreated tap water gives such good results that, after experimenting with hardening and softening compounds, the results are not worth the extra trouble. If you are going to bother then why not go all the way? Start with the analysis of your tap water, then add the precise quantity of salts to adjust this to hard or soft water.

2   Malted Barley

Barley is the source of the malt sugar used in brewing. Over the years much study has been done by farmers and Brewing Institutes to provide the right variety of barley. The barley is gathered in from the fields and left for what

is known as the resting period. This lasts for
about six weeks. No one has been able to
give a scientific reason for the resting of the
gathered grain, but nonetheless it is essential.
The raw barley grains are now sent to the
maltsters. The reason for malting is because
the raw barley grains contain starch which the
brewer wishes to have converted into a
fermentable sugar. The starch in the raw
barley is not readily fermentable in the natural
state but once the barley has been malted then
the starch is converted into a fermentable
sugar called maltose. The whole of the malting
system is scientifically controlled and it is the
high standard of this work, coupled with the
quality of the barley, that holds the key to the
quality of the beer. The malting process *can*
be reproduced at home but the resulting
quality of the malted barley would be very
poor and it is pointless for the home brewer
to try it.

Lastly, we come to the group of grains known
as adjuncts. These are grains used in
conjunction with malted barley by commercial
brewers. The main reason for the use of the
adjuncts is economy since these are cheaper
than malted barley but from the point of view
of the home brewer cost does not really matter
as the saving is so small. Oats were used
during the war when grains were in short

supply, but they were not found to be satisfactory. The grains most usually used at the present time are maize and rice. Not all brewers add adjuncts to their brews. Maize and rice have a secondary benefit in that, being low in soluble nitrogen, their addition to the grist helps in the easy clarification of the brew. Maize is reputed to give pale ales a much drier finish but do be careful not to use more than the stated quantity.

The point to note if you intend including adjuncts in your grist is to make sure that you buy *flaked* maize or rice. Before flaking the starch is not broken down, and if used in this state will not be of any use to you and will cause problems.

Some brewers like to make oatmeal stout, which is a stout with the particular flavour attributed to the oatmeal. Here again, ensure that you purchase flaked oatmeal. When using any of these adjuncts for inclusion in a mashed brew of beer, use only about 10% by weight in relation to malted barley. Adjuncts must be kept absolutely dry and free from moisture during storage.

3   Sugar

The sugar used by brewers can be divided into three categories, cane, invert and glucose.

In the early days of commercial brewing raw
sugar was used, but this proved unreliable
owing to the bacteria carried in sugar of this
type. More recently, refined sugar has been
generally used. For the home brewer refined
granulated sugar is as good as any and is, of
course, 100% pure. For making brown beers
or stouts it is quite safe to use small
quantities of brown sugar. The modern
brewers use invert sugar. This is sugar that
has been treated in a weak acid solution. As a
result of this treatment the sugar, which has
now been inverted, is immediately fermentable
by the yeast, whereas with granulated sugar an
enzyme in the yeast has to activate this
inversion before it can be fermented into
alcohol and carbon dioxide. By using invert
sugar the commercial brewer saves a little
time, which to him is money, but to the home
brewer is of little account. Invert sugar is
usually sold in 28 lb semi-solid blocks or in
solution. It is awkward for the home brewer to
handle, as in the semi-solid form it tends to go
runny.

Commercial invert sugars are flavoured with
caramel, the degree and style of flavour
depending on the style of beer to be made.
They also have the choice of many
proprietary sugars on the market, some of
which contain dextrin and are considered to

give more body and palate fullness to the finished beer. Glucose is a sugar prepared commercially by heating starch from potatoes, rice or maize with a weak acid solution. It is said that when this is used the beer has a drier finish, so it is more suitable for pale ale and lager. From the cost point of view glucose is dearer than granulated sugar for the home brewer. When deciding the amount of sugar to be added to your grist for mashing beers add about 15% by weight for pale beers and a little more for browns and stouts.

Lactose is a form of milk sugar and is unfermentable by brewer's yeast. It is used commercially in sweet stouts as a sweetener. Home brewers use it to sweeten their brown beers and stouts. Malt extract is the wort extracted from the malted barley and evaporated into a syrup. This is added to the commercial brew to help in the extraction from any badly modified malt grains. It is also added to the brew to help to give palate fullness to the beer. Malt extract is 100% fermentable in many cases. There are one or two malt extracts that are specially produced to contain a proportion of dextrins and this gives beer made from this style of malt extract more body and better head retention.

4   Hops

The hop is a vine-like climbing plant from
which the beer obtains its characteristic
bitterness. It came into prominence at the
beginning of the sixteenth century. In the
British Isles the main supplies of hops come
from Kent, Worcestershire and Herefordshire.
The two main varieties are Goldings and
Fuggles. There are some new types coming
on to the market and a large number of these
are hybrids of the two main varieties.
Goldings are supposed to have a more
delicate and subtle aroma and are best for
using in bitter beer, whilst Fuggles are mainly
used in browns and stouts. If you decide to
experiment with unusual varieties do be
careful since some varieties such as Bullion
have a very high bitterness and a much smaller
proportion should be used. Many continental
varieties of hops are now available to the
home brewer but you are advised to
experiment with small quantities until you find
out how they affect your brew. The hop adds
resins, which give beer its bitterness, and
essential oils which give the aroma of hops to
the beer. Unfortunately, as has been already
mentioned, many of the essential oils are lost
in the boiling so that some experts advocate
holding back up to a third of the hops until the
last quarter hour of the boiling. Others

suggest adding a few hops either just prior to pitching the yeast or during storage in cask at the end of the brew. It is a matter of personal preference. The tannin found in hops has a dual role in that it helps to prevent infection of the beer and also assists in its eventual clarification.

It is difficult for the layman to tell good hops from poor ones. There are, however, a few pointers. The smell should be clean and not cheesy. The colour should be pale green in the case of Fuggles and golden in the case of Goldings. Beware of hops that have an excess of brown leaves, for this indicates that they are old and oxidised and to be avoided. Obviously the commercial hop trade will have the first choice but there are nonetheless many good hops on the market. Once you discover a good quality hop buy it in bulk. It is no use buying 4 oz from a supplier and then, having adjusted your hop rate per gallon, going back for more and expecting the same quality. The turnover of most suppliers is such that they cannot guarantee that the second purchase is from the same packet of hops. I suggest that you buy from 6 to 12 months' supply at a time, after having previously assured yourself of the quality. Store in a cool, dry place. The cooler the store the better. Once you have adjusted your hop rate to your bulk purchase you should not need to vary it until the hops are used up.

The commercial brewers are continually experimenting with hop extracts to try and perfect them. There are several on the market available to the home brewer but I have yet to find a hop extract as good as the natural hop.

5   Yeast

There is no doubt that yeast is at the heart of all fermentation. Without it we should be lost. We are greatly indebted to Pasteur who, in 1859, was the first person to appreciate that yeast was a living organism and that it required special conditions in which to flourish. It was mainly due to his discoveries that brewers became aware of the opportunities that more scientific research would bring about. Others since Pasteur have done much in this field.

Yeast is a single-celled organism that needs sugar and vitamin B substances, in addition to several acids and ammonium salts in various degrees, in which to flourish. Fortunately malt wort is an ideal medium in which yeast can grow and multiply. The great danger to the brewer, or in fact the winemaker, is that yeast abounds in the atmosphere, and

there are many different strains of yeast.
The ones in the atmosphere are wild yeasts.
If these get into the wort they can have
damaging effects. One type of wild yeast will
give all the outward signs of a vigorous
ferment and yet the specific gravity of the
wort will not fall.

The way to avoid contamination by wild yeasts
is to have what is known as an active yeast
starter ready to put into the wort as soon as it
is cool enough, i.e. 58° to 60°F. The question
of what is a good yeast starter then arises.
Firstly, you must have a true strain of beer
yeast. Never use a baker's or a wine yeast or
your beer will lack quality and your yeast will
not settle hard on the bottom of the bottle.
For the scientifically minded the correct
name of the British top fermenting beer yeast
is *Saccharomyces cerevisiae*. The type of yeast
used in making lager is a different strain,
called *Saccharomyces Carlsbergensis*.

You can obtain *cerevisiae* yeast either by trying
a bit of persuasion at your local brewery,
or from the home brew suppliers. Many yeast
preparations are of a very high calibre and
come up to all requirements. You will soon
find by trial and error those that fall short of
the required standard. If the yeast is sold as a
top fermenting yeast then you should have a

good 'rocky head' on the top of your
fermenting wort between 12 and 24 hours after
pitching. As I have pointed out, the sooner
you can get your active yeast into your wort
the less chance of wild yeast spoilage.

On many of the yeast packets sold it is stated
that they can be introduced straight into the
wort without first making them into an active
yeast starter. Although it is true that this can
be done, I do not advise this method, as the
yeast has to build up its activity in the wort
and while this is happening the wort is still
prone to pick up any infection from the
atmosphere. It is much safer to have your
yeast starter really active for pitching into the
wort and so have your wort active and
protected that much more quickly. To prepare
your yeast starter all that is needed is a
one-pint vessel with not too small a mouth.
Fill this with one third of a pint of cold water,
stir in two or three dessertspoons of malt
extract, then add the contents of the yeast
packet or bottle. Stir the contents and place
the vessel in a warm place. Stir two or three
times daily for two days. By this time the yeast
should be really active. The reason I suggest a
vessel with a fairly large mouth is that beer
yeasts are generally more active than wine
yeasts and, if confined in a narrow space, the
carbon dioxide gas given off forces the yeast

up out of the container. As soon as your yeast starter is active, you are ready to prepare the wort for the pitching of the yeast.

The actual activity of the yeast follows a pattern. For the first few hours the yeast cells in the nutrient solution of the starter bottle or the wort take in the nutrients. They then start what is known as budding: they form cells and then divide and form other cells. This goes on at a fantastic rate. Carbon dioxide gas is given off and comes to the surface causing, in a brew using a top fermenting yeast, the rocky head previously described. It makes the wort look as if a packet of soap powder had been poured into the brew and stirred vigorously. The top of the wort is a mass of bubbles rising and falling. In a commercial brewery the rocky head can be as much as one and a half feet high. At home in, say, a five-gallon container the head will be about three to four inches. As the ferment proceeds the bubbles die down and the head looks more plastic as the yeast head thickens and becomes more solid.

After about two to three days the first yeast head should be skimmed off and thrown away, since this contains all the waste matter from the boil. A second head will form and from this you can obtain a yeast from which

to start your next brew, as long as you keep
the yeast in a refrigerator for not longer than
about seven days. After this period the yeast
tends to deteriorate and you could spoil your
next brew just by trying to save the price of
fresh yeast. I know that breweries use the
same yeast over and over again but they
employ chemists using microscopes and
other aids to ensure that their yeast is kept in
perfect condition until it is used.

Top fermenting yeast works or ferments best
at a temperature of around 58° to 60°F and it
cannot be too often repeated that every effort
should be made to keep your wort down to
this figure, to avoid yeast bite, which will
give your beer an acrid bitterness.

A vigorous, rousing stirring will help to
accomplish the fermentation by the yeast.
This is especially important when fermenting
out the high gravity beers, in particular barley
wine type beers. With these it may take quite a
considerable time to ferment down to the
required gravity. To avoid contamination of the
wort, I always advocate transferring the brew
into one-gallon jars, with airlocks fitted to
ensure that I can safely ferment down as low
as I require.

When making lager with a lager yeast the

temperatures are lower than the top yeast figures. In some of the continental breweries the lager is fermented over a much longer period and the temperature is as low as between 39° and 45°F. Lager is not an easy beer to make in the traditional style and many home brewers compromise by making a lightly hopped pale ale with a continental bottom yeast in conjunction with continental hops. By using these ingredients they get a reasonable resemblance to lager.

To sum up, use only authentic top fermenting yeasts for bitter beer, browns and stouts. For lagers use the continental bottom fermenting lager yeasts. If you do decide to skim off some of your yeast from the top of your wort to use again on your next brew, be very careful. Store the yeast in your refrigerator but do not try to store it for longer than one week. This warning only applies to the storing of a skimmed yeast. The yeast that you purchase in sealed packets or bottles will, of course, last for many months if stored correctly. But once it is opened the contents should be used up immediately. Never, on any account, use baker's yeast or a wine yeast to make beer.

6   Yeast Food

Yeast food is not generally needed in
beermaking as malt is an ideal medium for
fermentation. The only time that it might be
required would be in the fermentation of barley
wine, which is a brown beer of very high
alcoholic strength. As beer yeasts are not
normally called upon to ferment out very
high gravities you may experience difficulty in
getting the normal beer yeast to ferment out
barley wine, which often has a starting
gravity of 1.075. In this event, it may be
advantageous to add one of the vitamin B
complexes of yeast nutrient. This, coupled with
a vigorous stirring, should eventually reduce
the gravity.

7   Finings

Some beers will fall bright without the
addition of finings, but in most cases finings
are added to speed the process. Carrageen
moss or, as it is sometimes called, Irish moss,
is a form of seaweed and it is added to the
wort in the boiling stage to assist in the
eventual clarification of the beer. If you use the
natural moss do be careful not to add too
much, as this can have an adverse effect.
No more than four grains per gallon should be
added to the wort, about fifteen minutes prior

to the end of the boil. Irish moss is sometimes sold in liquid form under the name of auxiliary finings and these should be added according to the manufacturer's instructions. All bottled beers need to be fined prior to bottling. Many excellent fining agents are obtainable from winemakers' suppliers. Most of these have an isinglass base. Isinglass is the swimming bladder of the sturgeon and only the finest quality should be used. It must be cut with acid and will need the addition of metabisulphite to keep it from going sour.

5 Mashing at Home

To try to emulate the commercial brewer by making your beer by the same system that he uses is not as difficult as may first appear. The main difficulty is that the commercial brewer has at his disposal very sophisticated apparatus which enables him to control the temperature much more easily than the home brewer. There is one great advantage that the home brewer has, however, he can experiment with different compositions of grist and hop quantities until he has the brew exactly right for his own palate. The same person seeking to find a commercial beer to suit him has to shop around until he finds the nearest style.

Equipment

The most important utensil is a large mashing vessel. This can range from a large saucepan to a Burco type boiler. The larger the vessel the easier it is to make a large quantity of beer at any one time. It is much easier to mash your grist if you have gas as a heat source, for with electricity once you have the required heat for your liquor it is harder to switch off instantly and then to re-heat at a moment's notice. This can, of course, be got over by moving the saucepan off the hotplate when the required temperature has been reached and at the same time leave one hotplate at full heat in case you wish to bring up the temperature of the mash later in the mashing period. The minimum size saucepan is a two-gallon one. If you can possibly get a larger one so much the better. This brings me to an interesting phenomenon that seems to exist in home beer and winemaking circles. In most hobbies that the public enjoys, cost always seems to be the last consideration. If you join a camera club you will find that the most humble members pay enormous sums for most expensive cameras. Similarly, if you mix in tropical fish or philatelist circles, money, once again, seems to be no object. After many years of mixing with home wine- and beer-makers the moment you mention that an article of equipment is going to cost a few pounds, even though it is something that will be used year in and year out, they will raise their hands in horror as if you are suggesting that they buy the crown jewels. What is the reason for this strange outlook? I don't think that it is because the home brewer is any less interested in his hobby. I think the real reason lies in the advance publicity that the newcomer receives. Everyone tells him how cheaply every type of drink can be made and the whole emphasis is placed upon how cheap instead of on how good. Bear this in mind when you come to equip yourself for wine - or

beermaking. It is commonsense to tread
warily until you are certain that you are going
to continue with the hobby, but once you are
certain then I suggest that you equip yourself
with all the correct equipment regardless of a
certain cost. If you are not careful you will
find that for years you carry on making do
with poor equipment, and forget that for a few
pounds you can make your beermaking life so
much easier.

The next most important item is a good, large,
immersion-type thermometer. This is obviously
a must if you are going to check mashing
temperature. One about 12 inches in length is
ideal, larger if you wish, but certainly no
smaller. In fact, if you are wise you will
purchase two because nothing is more
frustrating than to be in the middle of mashing
a brew of beer and then accidentally to break
your thermometer. So play for safety and
have a spare one.

A large-size straining vessel is a great
advantage. You may, if you brew in large
quantities of over five gallons at a time, be
able to make a large and efficient piece of
apparatus yourself. If you have not got this
skill and want a readymade article I suggest
you go to a professional caterer's
establishment and purchase a wooden-sided

nylon sieve. I have found this type of sieve
(approximately 10 inches in diameter and
6 inches deep) invaluable, although a larger
size will be better still if you can find one.

A gallon-size funnel for the final straining is a
great asset. Naturally you will also require an
hydrometer and a trial jar. There are special
hydrometers for beer on the home brew market
but I have found that the usual wine
hydrometer is quite adequate for beermaking.
For fermentation nothing is better than the
five to ten-gallon plastic dustbin with a lid.
I suggest that you acquire also the same
number of gallon jars, airlocks and corks as
you are going to make gallon batches. That is
to say, if you usually make a five-gallon batch
then you will want at least five one-gallon jars.
A roll of kitchen paper makes an ideal filter
medium for filtering the wort. Make sure you
have a syphon tube of a good length with a
glass U-bend. This is all the equipment you
will need to mash beer in the same way as the
commercial brewer but, as I have already
mentioned, it will do no harm to have two of
everything.

Having collected all the necessary equipment
make sure that you keep it clean, dry and
sterile. Always use a plastic syphon tube
because you can see through it. If you use a

rubber tube there is the danger of earwigs concealing themselves unseen in the opaque rubber tube! Before we actually begin to try emulating the methods of the commercial brewer just one word of warning. Do not try too complicated a recipe or, as some people like to call a beer recipe, a formulation. Start with a nice simple one and, once you have mastered this and can get consistently good results then, and only then, should you try adding various adjuncts to your recipe or formulation. A simple recipe that I have used for many years to make a pale ale of similar style to a commercial Double Diamond is as follows:

2 lb crushed pale malted barley
2 dessertspoons medium dark, dried malt extract
1 oz crystal malt
¾ oz of hops
1 gallon water
Beer yeast

The first point to make is to remind you to buy your pale malted barley already crushed. The crushing of the malt grains is of prime importance in relation to the amount of extract that you are eventually going to extract from the grain when you mash. As I have previously mentioned, the commercial brewer goes to great lengths to grade and crush his malted barley so that he does not crush it so finely that it turns into flour nor so coarsely that the water cannot enter into the grains to extract the starch sugar. So, buy your malted barley *after* it has been professionally crushed by the maltsters. In this way it will be in the ideal condition for mashing.

The second important point is to ensure that your crushed malted barley is biscuit dry, in fact the moisture content should never rise above 2%. If it does rise above this figure the malt will be slack and you will have difficulties with extraction and clarification. As this dryness is of such primary importance I find it is better to buy crushed malted barley in 56 lb bags and store it myself. I only open the sack for sufficient time to take out the malt required for the particular brew and then seal the bags immediately. I appreciate that everyone will not wish to buy in such quantities, but it is always cheaper to buy in bulk and if you use 2 lb per gallon and brew beer continually you will soon get through a 56 lb bag. The remarks that I have made with regard to crushing and dryness apply just as much to the crystal and the patent black malts, although I do not suggest that you buy these in 56 lb bags as you will use much less of them.

We now come to the matter of your water or
liquor. If you live in a very soft water district
you could add up to 70 grains of calcium
sulphate (gypsum) and 10 grains of magnesium
sulphate. Failing this, you can buy one of the
proprietary salts available for hardening soft
water when making bitter beer. Of course if
you are a purist there is only one way to
prepare your water. Either get de-ionised or
distilled water and get a chemist to prepare
salts to bring it up to the requirements of
Burton well water. Or get your local water
analysed and then get salts precisely
prepared to make this up to the requirements
of Burton water. I have spoken with many head
brewers and the consensus of opinion is that
if you are only making small quantities, such
as five-gallon batches, it is more trouble than
it is worth to bother to try altering the
character of your liquor unless it is at the very
opposite range from what you desire.

For the home brewer ordinary granulated
white sugar is quite adequate for pale ales.

The yeast used for pale ales should always be
a top fermenting British beer yeast and always
prepared in a starter bottle. In this way you
start the yeast fermenting before adding it to
the beer. If you can get fresh yeast from a
brewery so much the better but, if not, you

can use one of the many very good beer
yeasts from the home beer suppliers. A fresh
yeast for each brew is recommended, as most
people do not have facilities for long storage
nor a microscope and knowledge to use it to
check the qualities of stored yeasts. If you
re-use the same yeast over and over again
there is a danger of getting wild yeast into
your brew and you may also experience
difficulty in attenuation and in clarification.
So do not spoil the ship for a ha'porth of tar.
This also applies to the buying of all supplies.
Always buy the very best ingredients available
even if they cost a little more. Remember that
you cannot make good beer from poor
quality ingredients.

Hops should be stored in a cool dry place.
My advice again is to buy in bulk and once
you have worked out by trial and error the
correct hop rate for this particular packet of
hops then you can standardise the quantity
as long as the bulk supply lasts. Also, of
course, the greater the quantity you buy the
cheaper the cost.
Now let us come to the making of your first
trial brew. Take your largest saucepan, fill it
with two gallons of water and heat it on the
gas until it reaches a temperature of 165°F.
This is the striking temperature. Into the
saucepan stir six pounds of crushed pale

malted barley, six dessertspoons of medium
dark dried malt extract and 2 oz of crushed
crystal malt. Now check the temperature of
the mash, which should have the consistency
of sloppy porridge. The temperature should be
about 150°F. If it is below this figure light the
gas and keep stirring until the temperature
reaches the desired figure of 150° or 152°F.
Switch off the gas, place a lid on the
saucepan and cover with any old blankets to
keep in the warmth. This insulates the
saucepan, and if you keep the doors closed to
maintain a warm atmosphere in the room you
should not have much heat loss. After 15
minutes remove the covers and lid and stir
the mash well for two or three minutes.
Check the temperature again and if necessary
reheat the brew whilst stirring. Put out the
gas, replace the lid and covers, and leave to
'stand on' for the next three-quarters of an
hour. Check the temperature again in about
half an hour in case any adjustment is
required. If you keep the saucepan well
covered and the room warm this is seldom
necessary. Just before the end of the
standing-on period heat six pints of water to
170°F.

I am not going to suggest that you mash for
two hours on the grain and then sparge for
two hours as the brewery seems to do. This is

not at all necessary, for you will have
extracted most of the fermentable matter in
the first hour. We do not have to obtain the
maximum extract that the commercial
breweries require. To them a few degrees of
gravity if the brew contains, say, 5000 gallons,
can mean a lot of money but to us, making a
three- to five-gallon brew, it is of no
consequence. So, as I have stated, the whole
of the mashing period in the saucepan should
be just one hour.

Remove the lid from your plastic dustbin and
across the top place two parallel wooden
runners such as one inch half-rounded
dowel rods. Upon these runners stand your
largest wooden-sided nylon sieve. Having got
your sieve into position over the dustbin
remove the saucepan covers and lid and fill
the sieve with the mash till it is almost level
with the top of the sieve sides. Let the wort
run through. Then wash the mash grains
through with the water you have heated to
170°F. I find that three pints washes through
the grain my 10 inch diameter sieve holds and
that two fillings of the sieve can cope with the
whole mash. By this method I fill the sieve
twice with the mash grain and wash each
sieve full through with three pints of water at
170°F. I usually sparge through a kettle. I can
see that commercial brewers, aiming for the

highest possible extract and dealing with a
great depth of grain, will need a fine sparge.
But for the home brewer I do not think this is
necessary, and as we cannot do it in
enclosed vessels the heat loss of the sparge
by means of a fine spray over a long period
would do more harm than good. In fact, if
you used more pounds of malt per gallon you
could, if necessary, do without the sparge
altogether.

Having washed through your mashed grain
return the collected wort to the saucepan and
add at least two thirds of your hops to the
saucepan. Bring to the boil and boil as fast as
you can for at least one hour. The more
vigorous the boil the better will be the results.
For the last fifteen minutes add the remaining
third of the hops and, if you are going to use
it, add at this stage the carrageen moss,
remembering that you add no more than four
grains per gallon. Boil on for the remaining
fifteen minutes, then strain the hopped wort
through the sieve. The hops retained in the
sieve can be sparged with a couple of pints of
hot water to wash through any sweet wort in
the hops. The wort is then put into the
coolest place, usually in the open air, to cool
quickly.

When the wort is cold, if the boiling has been
really effective the wort will stand bright and

clear but there will be a heavy deposit on the bottom of the container. Syphon the clear wort into a clean container, making sure that none of the deposit is carried over with the clear wort. The wort containing the deposit can now be filtered through filter paper and a large funnel into a gallon jar. The ideal medium to use for filter paper is a roll of kitchen paper. This will be found to be porous enough to let the clear wort through fairly quickly and at the same time will retain the brown sludge.

As soon as the wort is clear and cold take a specific gravity reading of the wort and add granulated sugar to bring the S.G. up to the required level. 2 oz per gallon adds 5 units. Whilst doing this it is well to remember that the commercial brewer of bitter beer usually keeps the amount of sugar to the rate of not more than 15% by weight of the total grist. It must be remembered that when you mash at 150° to 152°F there should be some dextrins in the wort, which will increase the gravity of the wort. With this in mind it will be quite possible to have a beer in which there is practically no residual sugar but which when finished has an S.G. of 1.006. So, when adding sugar, remember this point as you work out the alcoholic strength of the finished beer. I like to start my attenuation with the wort

adjusted to an S.G. 1.045. This usually
attenuates down to 1.005 to 1.006, the
remaining gravity being made up mainly of
dextrins.

Having adjusted the S.G., now is the time to
pitch your yeast. The temperature of the wort
at the time of pitching is of the greatest
importance and it is here that I think many
home brewers go wrong. They mistakenly have
their temperatures too high – near the 70°F
mark, whereas the most effective temperature
is between 58 and 60°F. Remember also that
the intense activity of the yeast will produce a
certain increase in the heat of the wort. So do
not ferment or attenuate in too warm a room.

For the first 24 hours stir the wort vigorously
whenever the opportunity arises (about five
or six times). After this a rocky head will form
and as it starts to settle skim off the early
yeast which will have waste matter and bits of
hops in it. After skimming give the wort
another good stir and then allow it to attenuate
towards finality. Here you can exercise a little
discretion. When the wort is within four or
five degrees of the desired finished gravity I
strain it off into one-gallon jars and insert an
airlock. The reason for this is that, since it is
a low alcohol product, beer is an easy prey
to bacterial infection. As soon as the specific

gravity falls low enough I like to exclude the
dangers from the air. Once in the gallon jars
the brew can be left to attenuate right down.
When fermentation stops leave the brew for a
couple of days in a cool place for the sediment
to settle and then syphon the beer from the
lees. The aim now is to have as little yeast
deposit as possible in the bottle. To this end
I add an isinglass-based beer fining. Any of
the proprietary brands on the market will do.

The brew with addition of the finings is now
returned to the gallon jars, which have
meanwhile been washed out, and the air
locks are reinserted. The gallon jars should
be left in a cool place for five to ten days,
depending on how well the brew clears. When
you are satisfied that the brew has cleared
sufficiently, you can again syphon off the
sediment into a clean bucket. From the
bucket you can partly fill your bottles with the
brew, having previously made sure that your
bottles are completely sterile, with clean
stoppers and new or sterilised rubber stopper
rings. When this is done you have to add your
priming sugar, to give the yeast some sugar
from which to create the carbon dioxide gas
required to make the beer gaseous. I use a
sugar solution obtained by boiling one pound
of sugar in half a pint of water until dissolved
and then allowed to go cold. To each partly

filled bottle of beer I add one teaspoonful of
this sugar syrup. I then fill each bottle with
beer until it is within three-quarters of an inch
off the bottom of the stopper. Screw up the
stoppers tightly or affix the crown corks and
move the bottles to a warm place for a few
days until the secondary fermentation has
occurred and the beer is gassy. After, say,
ten days, release the stopper on one of the
bottles; if gas escapes and bubbles rise in the
bottle immediately reseal. The bottle and the
whole brew is now ready for storage.

Here again we come to one of the most
neglected aspects of home brewing; that is
the maturation of the beer. In the breweries
they leave their natural fermentation beers in
cask for two months before bottling. Most
people would find this a little difficult to do,
but if you have the cellarage and the other
facilities it is well worth trying. For the rest
of us, whilst we cannot store for long prior
to bottling, we can store our primed bottles,
once they are gassy, in a cool dry place for at
least two months. This will make a great
difference in the flavour, the condition, and
the head retention of the beer.

This system of mashing is basically the same
for all styles of beers. The only difference will
be in the mashing temperature when making

a brown ale or a stout. Even this is a matter of
personal opinion and taste, but some home
brewers prefer to have a little less dextrin in
their browns and to mash at about 146° to
148°F. When it comes to the bottling of
brown beer or sweet stouts an addition of
lactose has to be made to give these beers
their finished sweetness. This is a matter of
personal taste. If you like your browns and
stouts fairly sweet, then I suggest the
addition of lactose at the rate of 4 oz per
gallon but this can obviously be adjusted to
your own requirements. Bring the 4 oz lactose
to the boil in a cup of water, add to the bulk
gallon of beer and stir well just prior to bottling.
The reason for the heating is to ensure more
even distribution. It must be appreciated that
the lactose is non-fermentable, so that after
its addition to the bulk you will still need to
add one teaspoonful of sugar syrup as a
priming agent, as already described.

6 Malt Extract Beer

I think it is correct to say that more home brewed beer is made from malt extract than in any other way. Malt sugar is extracted from barley grains by mashing it in water at a certain temperature and then the water is evaporated until a heavy syrup is formed. The majority of the malt extracts sold by the suppliers has been extracted at about 140°F and as a result it is 100% fermentable. But there are one or two that have been specially extracted to contain some dextrins. These are the unsweetened tasteless gummy substances that give beer a better body. Malt extracts with dextrins in them do not ferment out to S.G. 1.001 or 1.000. These will ferment down to 1.008 or lower but the degrees of gravity shown above 1.000 will be not fermentable sugar but dextrins.

To explain this more clearly. If you start fermenting a non-dextrin malt extract brew at S.G. 1.045, the brew will ferment right down to S.G. 1.000. If the brew is made from one of the special malt extracts containing dextrins, however, it will ferment down only to S.G. 1.008 and then cease, as no more sugar will be contained in the wort. The eight degrees of gravity will be made by the dextrins. It is, therefore, important when making beer from malt extract to know whether it contains dextrins. The suppliers always note on the tin if it does contain dextrins.

Malt extract comes in two styles. The dried malt extract is in powder form and is very susceptible to moisture. If left in a damp atmosphere it will turn into a solid lump resembling toffee. It will be quite usable in this state but a little messy to handle. It comes in three colours. The pale, which is off-white to pale fawn, is used for pale ales; the second type is the colour of dried egg, or slightly darker in colour than the pale extract. It looks fairly light in colour but when dissolved it turns the liquor quite dark, in fact a much darker brown than would be expected by the colour of the dried extract. There is a third dried extract which is chocolate brown in colour. This, like the medium dark malt extract, is used as a colouring medium, usually for stouts.

The more common form of malt extract is, of course, in the syrup form. It is available in various styles, the darker being used for the brown beers. There are many different brands of malt extract upon the market and each home brewer must experiment and choose the particular extract to suit his own palate. The basic quantity is 1 lb of malt extract to 1 gallon of water to 1 oz of hops. All these

quantities can be varied to suit the individual
taste of each brewer. Small additions of
crystal malt or maize may also be added to
each gallon to vary the style and flavour of the
brew. Although malt extract as a main base
for brewing is not recommended for making
high quality beer it is by far the most popular
way of making beer at home. The malt
extract is simply added to the hops and water
and boiled for from one to two hours. The wort
is then strained from the hops and more water
and some sugar is added to adjust the
quantity of liquor and its gravity. The ideal
starting gravity for strong bitter beer should
not exceed S.G. 1.045 to 1.050. If it does the
beer will be too strong in alcohol for normal
consumption. From the point of view of
economy it is better to purchase your hops
and malt extract in bulk. The larger the
quantity the cheaper it becomes. Just one
word of warning in regard to the malt extract.
If you only make a small quantity of beer at a
time do not buy too large a quantity of malt
extract as it is not good to keep a container of
malt extract nearly half empty for months on
end.

It may seem a very simple point but many
home brewers, when I suggest that they buy
their malt extract in bulk, ask how can they
weigh out, say, two pounds without making a

mess. They feel that they have to pour two pounds of extract into a jar and then weigh it. This is, of course, quite wrong. All you need to do is to weigh the container of malt and note its weight. Then pour what you think is two pounds into your saucepan. You can check how much has been removed simply by reweighing the container of malt extract to ensure that it is two pounds lighter. This is important when taking two pounds from, say, a seven- or fourteen-pound container of malt extract.

Most malt extracts, in my opinion, seem to give the resultant beer a slight tang peculiar to the extract used but as so many thousands of home brewers do not seem to notice or mind this flavour, perhaps it is wrong of me to dwell upon it. When using malt extract you can add crystal malt for flavour or, in the case of brown beer, patent black malt and colouring at the same time as your hops. When you make brown beer or stout remember that these are only lightly hopped. For those who find this process too difficult there is on the market a great range of malt extracts that have been hopped and flavoured for the different styles of beers and all the home brewer has to do is to add sugar and water and a beer yeast. Here again it is a matter of trial and error to get the brand that suits your particular palate.

A certain amount of caution is required. If you
take 1 lb of malt extract and 1 oz of hops to
1 gallon of water as a basic standard, with the
knowledge that the amount of malt
extract or hops could be increased or
decreased above or below this figure by about
half yet still make a reasonable drink, you will
have what are the extreme limits of the range
of these ingredients. That is to say no less
than $\frac{1}{2}$ lb of malt extract per gallon nor less
than $\frac{1}{2}$ oz of hops (Fuggles or Goldings) per
gallon. I mention this because I have seen
some suppliers who are prepared to suggest
that 1 lb of malt extract can be made into five
gallons of beer. I regret that I cannot agree
with these rather optimistic claims. I know
that as long as you add plenty of sugar you
will get an alcoholic drink but it will not taste
very much like beer. So do be careful when
buying these composite malt extracts that
you are not expected to try to make 1 lb of
malt extract into more than two gallons of
beer.

Beer Packs

These beer packs are similar to the hopped
malt extracts. A packet contains sufficient
ingredients to make a given quantity of beer.
They are obviously for the person who does
not want to experiment but prefers to have

everything done for him (even if it does cost more) and does not mind having little opportunity to vary the taste of the beer. Nonetheless, there must be a lot of people brewing this type of beer, as there is a very heavy sale for these packs. Here again it must be a matter of trial and error to find which supplier gives the best value for money. One obvious point is that the pack with the greatest quantity of malt extract per gallon of beer should be the best value. No doubt some of these packs make very excellent beer but I do not feel that they would have much success as competition beers. One of the difficulties in using malt extract or beer packs is to make a beer that has a good close-knit head and, more important, has the ability to retain this head. Artificial additives can be put into the brews to assist head retention but I do not recommend them. Just one tip: to avoid difficulty in fermentation whichever system you use, whether malt extract already hopped or a beer pack, make sure that you boil your ingredients in water and then allow them to cool before adding your yeast. Make sure if you buy a beer pack that the yeast included is a top fermenting yeast. You will see why as soon as you make your first brew.

How to Make Malt Extract Brews

1   Into your saucepan put malt extract,
hops, any additives such as crystal malt or
maize or patent black malt and colouring.

2   Add water and bring to boil. Make sure at
the beginning that it cannot boil over. To avoid
this stir until the hops are well saturated with
the wort, then adjust so that the wort boils
vigorously without boiling over.

3   Strain the wort from the hops and wash
the hops through with a couple of pints of
water, then leave the wort to cool.

4   Syphon off the clear wort and strain the
remainder through some kitchen paper.

5   Collect the wort into a fermenting vessel
and adjust the quantity by adding water and
the gravity by adding sugar.

6   Pitch the yeast when the temperature of
the wort is 58°F (if possible).

7   Stir well and stir again in twelve hours.

8   When the yeast rises to the surface of
the brew skim it off.

9   Stir well and allow the yeast to form on top of the brew,

10   If ordinary malt extract has been used, ferment out (or to use brewers' terminology, attenuate out) to a specific gravity of 1.000.

11   To ensure that your brew does not become acetified, I suggest that after the yeast has fermented out nearly all the sugar, i.e. to a specific gravity of say 1.006, you put the beer into gallon jars and insert airlocks so that the ferment finishes off without being over-exposed to the atmosphere. You must, of course, skim off the yeast before doing this.

12   Leave the brew in gallon jars until a few days after fermentation is completed and the beer is clearing.

13   Syphon the beer off the sediment, wash out the gallon jars and return the brew to the jars.

14   Into each gallon jar of beer stir in two teaspoons of proprietary beer finings.

15   Reinsert the airlocks and place the gallon jars in a cool place for from five to ten days, to allow the beer to clear.

16   Syphon the beer from the sediment and
bottle it in screwtop bottles, adding one
teaspoon of sugar syrup per bottle (syrup is
1 lb sugar dissolved in $\frac{1}{2}$ pint of water).

17   Screw up the stoppers tightly and store
the bottles in a warm place for the beer to
become gassy.

18   When the beer is gassy it is ready for
drinking, but will improve greatly if matured
for at least one to two months in a cool
place.

If screwtop bottles are not available,
ordinary beer bottles and crown corks may be
used instead.

But remember: no matter how well you make
your beer it will never be better than the
ingredients from which it is made will allow.

Draught Beer

This is beer stored in a bulk container that
has had priming sugar added. The beer is
slightly gassy but usually not so much so as
bottled beer. The containers for draught beer
can be obtained from the beermaking
suppliers. They must be strong enough to
stand a little pressure and have a tap fitted

from which to pour the beer. Many home
brewers have their own sophisticated
systems. Some even store their beer in casks
and draw it up through beer engines. This
expertise is beyond the scope of the beginner.
The equipment is expensive and a certain
amount of engineering knowledge is
required.

Bottling

Beer bottles are obviously the best type of
bottle to use, but I have been making beer for
more than twenty years and during this time I
have used many lemonade bottles and never
had one burst. I would certainly draw the line
at just any screwtop bottle unless it had been
made to withstand the normal CO_2 pressure
required for carbonated drinks. Make sure
that your pressure rings inside the stopper
are clean and in good condition. Make sure
that the stoppers themselves are clean. There
are four types of bottle stoppers.

1   The central screw type used for many
years on beer bottles but now going out of
production.

2   The overall plastic screw stopper used on
lemonade bottles.

3   The plastic 'reseals' that are sold by home brew suppliers and can be used over and over again. They are simply pressed over the top of the bottle.

4   Last but not least there are the crown corks. These can be clamped on with a simple tool costing around sixty pence but for £2 a machine does the job more quickly and easily.

For competition purposes screw tops with a central thread, plastic 'reseals' or crown tops are usually allowed. At most of the shows of any size the stipulation is brown or green beer bottles only. Make sure that you wash your bottles well with a bottle brush and use one of the many proprietary brands of sterilising liquids on the market. Wash out the bottles thoroughly and drain them dry before use.

7 Faults and How to Correct Them

Impure Water

If you use the water from the tap you should have no difficulty regarding its pureness. Well water is more doubtful and should not be used until you have consulted your local water authorities.

Set Mash

This is usually due to the grist being crushed too finely. This could happen if instead of buying your grains already crushed you try doing it yourself with the aid of an electric kitchen grinder, which tends to grind too finely. Always use the best quality grains. The advice about quality applies to all ingredients. Keep your raw grain within the limits I have stated. If you are in doubt about the quality of malted barley, then add up to 10% of a highly diastatic malt extract to your mash. Most malt extracts sold to home brewers come within this category.

Slow Fermentation

The usual causes are:

1   Poor and impoverished yeast. To avoid this use a fresh yeast for each brew and ensure that it is a beer yeast and not a wine

or a baker's yeast. Make a starter bottle of
yeast to ensure that the ferment gets off
quickly to a good start.

2   Poor quality malted barley, lacking in
nutrients. Always buy the best quality grains.
If in doubt add yeast food.

3   Wort out of balance through too much
malto-dextrins and dextrins.

4   Too much nitrite and nitrate in the liquor.
No more than 5 grains per gallon can be
permitted and using pure tap water will ensure
that this proportion is not exceeded.

5   Too low a fermenting or attenuation
temperature. This can be countered by moving
the beer to a warmer temperature. The best
temperature is between 58° and 60°F for top
fermenting yeasts. A lower temperature when
making lager is permissible.

6   Too high a hop content. This can
sometimes occur when making a strong,
highly-hopped beer. There is a lack of the
usual yeasty head. Vigorous and regular
rousing by stirring will overcome this problem.

7   Deterioration of the yeast by frequent
re-use bringing a change in the character of

the yeast. Do not use the yeast more than twice before renewing the strain.

Yeast Bite

This is an intense, acrid bitterness in the finished beer. Sometimes it is confused with over-hopped beer. Once tasted, the acrid flavour of this yeast bite is always recognised in the future. It is caused by adding too much yeast to the wort. The residue of yeast and waste matter, which gathers in the early stage of the fermentation around the periphery of the bucket at yeast level, should be wiped off with a damp cloth.

Flat Beer, Lack of Condition and Head Retention

A flat beer is sadly lacking in flavour. It looks and tastes dead. The lack of bead or bubbles rising is due to lack of condition. This is caused by either faulty stoppering allowing the gas to escape or to lack of priming at the bottling stage. If the beer has been well-stoppered and has had priming added, but is still lacking in condition, then you will usually find, in the case of bitter beer, a bitter-sweet finish. This shows that the bottle has not had time to mature after sealing and the priming sugar has not had time to be converted into CO_2 by the yeast.

The lack of a good creamy head in bottled beer is rather harder to cure. I find that most brews from malt extract lack this quality and only longer maturation can remedy the situation. To obtain a really good head retention you must mash your brew from grain. You must, of course, have the CO_2 gas generated in the bottle by the action of the yeast on the priming sugar and not by carbonation. The presence of dextrins in the beer undoubtedly helps in head retention. Mash at 152°F to obtain these. Hop resins also assist in head retention. The use of slack malt can have a very adverse effect. Your malted barley must be biscuit-dry. Anything less than this will bring trouble. A long maturation period of two to three months is also beneficial in getting good head retention. Last, but not least, always pour your beer into clean dry glasses that have not been previously washed in detergent.

Above all else, take care. Do not try to cut corners or use inferior ingredients to save a few minutes or a few coppers. Whatever beer you make should be better than what you can buy so do not try to cut the cost except by bulk buying.

Cloudiness

This is usually due to an excess of yeast in the

beer and can be removed by fining with a commercial fining a week before bottling. Mashed brews will sometimes go cloudy if chilled too long in the refrigerator but when taken out they clear as the temperature rises. It is admittedly a little more difficult to get a mashed brew as star-bright as with a malt extract brew. Remember that beer these days is sold largely upon its eye appeal and not its taste while, with homemade beer, although a slight haze is not strictly desirable, the far superior taste of the beer often makes up for this slight defect.

8 Competitive Beer-making

Each year the number and variety of beer classes in the shows around the country are on the increase. If you wish to compete successfully in these shows there are several points that must be borne in mind. Whether it is a big national show or a small club show, you must read the schedule carefully. Decide if you have any beer that fits the description of the classes in the schedule. If you have beer that you feel is good enough and is of a type similar to those mentioned then you must ensure that your beer is bottled and stoppered according to the rules.

In the larger shows the classes are described so that the type of beer is fairly easy to recognise, e.g. Bitter Beer, Burton type. This is obviously a bitter beer, fairly well hopped, with a fairly strong alcohol content. The commencing S.G. would have been 1.045 – 1.050. Your beer to fit this class should be similar in style to one of the nationally produced beers of Burton-on-Trent, such as Double Diamond, Bass or Worthington. These beers are different in colour and flavour but have a close resemblance in body and bitterness. If a schedule lists Irish Stout, then the judge will expect a dark brown stout with the characteristic bitterness of Guinness. Sweet stout should be similar to Mackesons Stout. In the case of brown beer it is a little more difficult as there are no nationally known brown beers that cover the whole of the country in the same way as the stouts. The Northern style of brown beer is the Newcastle Brown. This is dark amber, with a sweet bitterness not usually found in brown beers. The more traditional brown beer is dark brown, with a sweet finish on the palate. The only way a home brewer can satisfactorily produce this sweetness is to stir a little lactose In to the finished beer prior to bottling. The amount of sweetness required can be obtained by boiling three to four ounces of lactose in a half pint of water until it is dissolved and then stirring this into each gallon of brown beer. The beer will still have to be primed in the normal way, as the lactose is non-fermentable. The same treatment can be given to sweet stouts.

It is almost impossible for a home brewer to make a gallon of beer of show quality and be certain of success. The easiest way to obtain your show beer is to adopt the following policy. Every time you make a brew of beer, bottle at least three bottles to the recognised show standard of correctness and label them accordingly. At a later date when this particular brew is matured, taste and evaluate it for clarity, condition (this is the amount of gas or carbonation in the beer), head

retention, bouquet and flavour. Having tasted
and weighed up dispassionately the quality of
your beer, then mark the two remaining
show-style bottles of this particular brew
according to how you judged them. You must
not let the fact that it is a brew of your own
making cloud your judgment.

If you adopt this system, then when a show
comes along you can pull out three or four
bottles of beer of different brews and re-judge
them. From these you enter the duplicate of
the bottle that you select as your best.

From the shows I have judged around the
country I find that the biggest fault is lack of
condition. When you open a bottle of beer and
pour a third of the contents into a clean dry
glass the bead of bubbles should arise and
continue for about half an hour. So many of
the beers I have judged are almost flat at the
time of pouring and the bead ceases to rise
after a couple of minutes. The second fault,
stemming to a certain extent from the first
failure, is lack of head retention. This is more
difficult to remedy than the first fault. Lack of
condition will alter completely the taste of
your beer, so you can appreciate that it is
most important to have good condition. It is
very simple to achieve this and failure is due
to lack of priming. If, before the beer is bottled,

you make sure that the residual sugar has been fermented out, then just prior to bottling add one teaspoonful of priming syrup (1 lb of sugar to $\frac{1}{2}$ pint of water). If the beer is primed with this and given time to work out, you should not have any difficulty in the condition of your beers. Head retention is more difficult to achieve and is not easily obtained in malt extract beers. Home brewers who mash their grain should, however, get a good head retention with grain beers that are well matured.

The following is how a National judge awards points when judging beer.

Bottling – 2 points
There should be $\frac{1}{2}$ to $\frac{3}{4}''$ air space between the beer and the stopper. Labels should conform to those laid down in the schedule. Check stoppers, closures and sealing rings for cleanliness. This last point also applies to bottles both inside and out. All old beer labels must be removed.

Condition and Clarity – 4 points
The yeast deposit on the bottom of the bottle should be firm and light. When opened, the deposit should remain firm on the bottom of the bottle. When poured into a dry glass the beer should have a good head retention. The

white layer of foam or bubbles that form the
head should sit on the surface of the beer and
stay there. It should be very close-knit,
resembling a cream, rather than having large
open bubbles. A close-weave bead should be
rising from the bottom of the glass and the
beer should be star-bright and free from any
haze.

Bouquet – 4 points
This will depend on the style of beer but it
should be clean and appetising. It should be
well balanced and representative of its type.

Taste – 20 points
This is where most points are gained (or lost).
The flavour must be well balanced according
to the style of beer. It should be fresh and
clean without over-acidity, over-bitterness or
over-sweetness and without any trace of
'off-flavours'.

Beer Styles

Pale ale, sometimes called light ale. A bitter
beer similar in style to dinner ale with a
starting gravity of about 1.030. It should be
clean and light on the palate and not too
hoppy in flavour.

Indian pale ale or Burton type. A bitter beer
more hopped in flavour than light ale, with a

starting gravity of around 1.040. Fuller-bodied than light ale, with a fuller malty flavour. Should be well-balanced and clean on the palate.

Brown Beer

There is no national beer with which home brewed brown ale can be compared, but its colour should be brown, although this can range from amber to dark brown. The degree of sweetness can vary but there should be an underlying residual sweetness. This is gained by the use of lactose. It is lightly hopped beer.

Sweet Stout

Heavier In fullness and flavour than a brown beer but still with an underlying sweetness. It may have an oatmeal flavour. A heavy, sweet beer.

Irish Stout

Similar in style to a Guinness. A heavy stout with a full flavour and a characteristic bitterness underlying the flavour. Should have a creamy, close-knit head.

Barley Wine

Not often seen in schedules. This is a heavy, sweet beer, very high in alcohol. Full-flavoured, but slightly more bitter than would normally be expected from a brown

beer. Often has a starting gravity of 1.080.
You may find difficulty in getting this beer to
ferment out and it may need regular rousing
to get the yeast to work.

Lager
This is light-bodied and coloured, with a very
delicate hop flavour. A fairly high starting
gravity of 1.050 is essential. A lager yeast
(bottom fermenting) should always be used.
This is a beer that is difficult to imitate, as it
should be fermented out very slowly at very
low temperatures. When made from grain
brewers use what is known as the
'decoction', a process that is too complicated
to deal with here. It involves taking quantities
out of the mash tun and reheating it to a
higher temperature, prior to reintroducing it
to the mash tun. It is not easy for the amateur
to imitate. The nearest we can get is a light-
flavoured, light ale style, but with higher
alcohol content. Continental hops such as
Hallertau or Saar can be obtained in this
country.

The styles that I have specified are mainly for
competitions. It is obvious that some people
like their beer to their own taste. Remember
that because a particular brew of beer was
successful at one show it does not necessarily
follow that it will win at the next show.

Judges are human and what will please one
may not suit another. But perhaps the most
important point is that the winning beer is
only the best of the beers in that particular
competition. So do not be surprised if a
winner does not repeat its success. To show
successfully you have to be completely
honest with yourself when appraising your
own efforts. Do not be satisfied with anything
short of perfection, since the judge will be just
as hard to please. Do not be discouraged if
you do not win the first show that you enter
but persevere at other shows until the first
comes round again.

9 Recipes

If you have read and understood the various methods of beermaking laid down in the pages of this book, you should not need recipes. For those readers who still lack confidence in their own ability, however, I have included some basic recipes. The quantities given can be varied to suit the individual palate of each brewer.

At the risk of being repetitive I should like once again to draw your attention to some of the salient facts of brewing. With the best techniques and the best recipes in the world you will still fail if you buy ingredients that are not of the highest quality. In regard to malt extracts there are many brands upon the market, including one or two that contain dextrins. Remember that those containing a high dextrin content will not ferment right down to zero. I have my own personal preference in malt extracts but it would be unfair to state it here. Try the various brands until you find the make that best suits your palate. Once you have decided on the malt extract that you like best, then I suggest that you buy it in bulk. The size of your bulk purchase will depend to a certain extent upon the amount of beer you make. If you are making around three gallons per week I would suggest that you buy 28 lb of malt extract at a time. If you make less than this, then 14 lb containers are the ideal size. Malt extract tends to deteriorate when left in half-empty containers for months on end so if you only make beer occasionally then buy your malt extract as you use it.

When mashing beer with pale malted barley, purchase your malted barley in the crushed state if at all possible and then store it in airtight containers. The exclusion of damp is of paramont importance. Hops can vary greatly from packet to packet so that, once you find a supplier with a good quality hop, buy in bulk. In this way you will obtain a continuity of hop quality. The hops must also be stored carefully. Find a cool dry place and once again make sure that all air is excluded. If you intend making lager then I suggest that you use the continental hops such as Saar or Hallertau, in conjunction with a lager yeast.

For all other beer use a pure strain British top fermenting yeast. Do not use the yeast more than twice before renewing it and store it in a refrigerator between brews. Do not be afraid to experiment and vary the quantities used in your recipe until you get it to your satisfaction. Broadly, the rule is to use additional hops for more bitterness – and vice versa. For more alcohol use more sugar and for a more malty flavour use more malt

extract. Reduce quantities for the opposite
effect.

1   RECIPES FOR BEER MADE BY MASHING MALTED BARLEY

Burton Type Bitter

1 gallon water
2 lb pale crushed malted barley
2 oz dried malt extract (medium dark)
1 oz Golding hops
6 oz sugar (approximately)
Top fermenting yeast

Method
Heat water to 165°F in a large saucepan. Then
put the malted barley and malt extract into the
saucepan and stir until the mash is well
mixed. Check the temperature and maintain it
at 152°F. Replace the lid on the saucepan and
cover it with old blankets to insulate the
saucepan. Stir twice in the first half hour, on
each occasion checking the temperature to
make sure that it is maintained at 152°F. If it
falls below this then reheat, stirring at the same
time until 152°F is regained. If the saucepan
has been well covered with blankets there
should be little danger of this happening.
Keep the mash undisturbed at 152°F for the
second half hour. (The mash has now been at

152°F for one hour.) At the completion of
the hour's mashing strain through a large
kitchen sieve (wooden-sided is best). Then
sparge by washing over the grain with water
at 165°F (three pints of sparge water to each
two pounds of grain used). Return all the liquor
to the saucepan and boil vigorously for an
hour and a half with the hops. Keep a third
of the hops back until the last fifteen minutes
of the boil, before adding them to the
saucepan. Strain off the hops and stand the
wort to cool. The quicker it cools the better.

When the wort is cold the waste and protein
matter which have coagulated in the boil will
settle at the bottom of your container. The rest
of the wort will be clear. Syphon off the clear
wort into your fermenting vessel. The wort that
is cloudy at the bottom of the cooling vessel
can be strained through a funnel into a gallon
jar, using kitchen paper as the filter medium.
The cleared wort is added to the wort already
syphoned into the fermenting vessel. Check to
ensure that the temperature is around 60°F
and check the specific gravity with an
hydrometer. Add sufficient water and sugar
to bring one gallon to a starting gravity of
1.040. Make quite sure that the sugar has
been thoroughly dissolved prior to taking the
reading. Maintain the temperature of the
wort at 60°F and then pitch in a starter bottle

of top fermenting beer yeast or, if using
brewery yeast, a piece the size of a small egg.
Stir in and maintain the temperature at 58° to
60°F or as near as is possible. Stir at frequent
and regular intervals for the first 12 to 24
hours.

On the third day skim off the top yeast and
wipe away the deposit around the edge of the
vessel at yeast level. Leave to ferment down to
about S.G. 1.008, then put the beer into gallon
jars and insert airlocks. Once this stage is
reached the beer can be left to ferment right
out without any worry of acetification. When
beer has completely fermented out, syphon off
the sediment, wash out the gallon jars and
return the beer to them. Add two teaspoons
of beer fining to each gallon jar and stand
them in a cool place until the beer clears. Then
syphon off the sediment and bottle into clean
screw-top bottles, adding one teaspoonful of
sugar syrup to each bottle. Store for at least
two months for the best results.

Brown Beer

1 gallon of water
1½ lb malted barley
3 oz crystal malt
2 oz black malt
6 oz dried malt extract (medium-dark)

$\frac{1}{2}$ oz hops
4 oz lactose
Top fermenting yeast

Raise water to 165°F, add all the grain and
malt extract and proceed mashing as before,
but at a temperature of 149°F. Follow the same
procedure as before until the bottling stage.
Prior to bottling heat the lactose in half a pint
of water until it is dissolved. Stir the dissolved
lactose into the gallon of beer. Stir well and
then bottle, priming in the normal way.

Irish Stout

$1\frac{1}{2}$ lb malted barley
4 oz black malt
2 oz burnt raw barley
8 oz dried malt extract (medium-dark)
1 gallon water
$\frac{1}{2}$ oz hops
Top fermenting yeast

Method as above, except that no lactose is
used.

Lager Style

1 gallon water
$1\frac{1}{2}$ lb malted lager barley
4 oz pale malt extract

4 oz flaked maize
¾ oz hops (Saar or Hallertau variety)
Lager yeast

Method

It is too complicated for the amateur to mash
the continental system called 'decoction'.
Instead, mash in the normal style, as given
for strong bitter beer, i.e. for one hour at
152°F. The method is the same as for bitter
beer, but use a continental yeast which is
bottom fermenting. For real success this
should be fermented out at a very low
temperature, between 45° and 50°F. Most
home brewers may be content to use the
normal fermenting temperature of 58° to 60°F.
Boil clear and bottle as for bitter beer.
Starting gravity about 1.050.

Barley Wine

1 gallon water
4 lb pale malted barley
2 oz crystal malt
12 oz dried malt extract (medium-dark)
¾ oz Golding hops
Top fermenting beer yeast
Yeast food

Mash at 150°F and proceed as for other
mashed brews. The attenuation (fermentation)

will be long and slow and the wort will need
to be agitated during the ferment to keep the
specific gravity from falling. This is a very
strong ale and should be drunk in small
quantities and with caution.

II. RECIPES FOR MAKING BEER BY USING MALT EXTRACT

Brown Beer

1 gallon water
1 lb malt extract
4 oz crystal malt
4 oz dried malt extract (medium-dark)
6 oz granulated sugar
$\frac{1}{2}$ oz hops
Beer yeast
4 oz lactose

Method
Place all the ingredients except the yeast into
a saucepan containing one gallon of water.
Bring to the boil and boil vigorously for one
hour (at least). Strain off the hops. When the
wort is cold add enough water and sugar so
that, when stirred into the wort, you have a
gallon with a gravity of 1.040. Add yeast and
stir well. After 24 hours skim off the top yeast
and wipe around the vessel at yeast level.
Ferment down to about S.G. 1.008 and then

syphon off into a gallon jar and insert an airlock. Allow to ferment right out. Then syphon off the lees, wash out the gallon jar and refill with the beer. Add two teaspoons of fining to each gallon jar, replace the airlock and stand the jar in cool place to clear. After about 5 days syphon off the sediment. Add lactose after dissolving it in half a pint of water. Bottle in the usual way, adding one teaspoonful sugar syrup per bottle. Like all beers it improves with keeping.

Bitter Beer

1 lb malt extract
1 gallon water
2 oz crystal malt
2 oz dried malt extract (medium-dark)
1 oz Golding hops
Beer yeast

Method
Make as preceding recipe but exclude the lactose.

Stout

1 gallon water
1 lb malt extract
4 oz patent black malt
2 oz crystal malt

4 oz burnt raw barley (torrified barley)
½ oz hops
Beer yeast
4 oz dried malt extract (medium-dark)
6 oz sugar

Method as for brown beer but exclude lactose.

Oatmeal Stout

1 gallon water
1 lb malt extract
4 oz flaked oatmeal
4 oz dried malt extract (medium-dark)
6 oz sugar
½ oz hops
Beer yeast

Method as for brown beer.

Barley Wine

1 gallon water
1 lb malt extract
1 lb dried malt extract (medium-dark)
2 oz crushed patent black malt grain
6 oz demerara sugar
¾ oz hops (Fuggles)
¼ teaspoonful yeast food
4 oz lactose
Top-fermenting beer yeast

Method

Boil all the ingredients, except the yeast and
yeast nutrient, in one gallon of water for one
hour. Strain off the hops and, when cold, add
water to make up the gallon and adjust specific
gravity by adding demerara sugar to bring it
to 1.075. Add yeast and yeast food, stir
regularly for five days, then syphon into gallon
jar and continue to ferment at 60°F until the
S.G. falls to around 1.014 or as low as you
can get it. With such a high starting gravity
the brew will need plenty of agitation and
plenty of time, even months, to reduce the
S.G. to the correct level. This beer will improve
with keeping. Bottle, adding priming and
lactose as for brown beer.